PORTSMOUTH PAST AND PRESENT

Compiled and photographed
by
ANTHONY TRIGGS

Ensign
PUBLICATIONS

Published by Ensign Publications,
2, Redcar Street, Shirley, Southampton SO1 5LL

British Library Cataloguing in Publication Data

Portsmouth past and present.
1. Portsmouth (Hampshire)—History
I. Triggs, Anthony
942.2′792′0222   DA690.P8

ISBN 1 85455 009 8

Design Brian Iles

Phototypeset by Inforum Ltd, Portsmouth

Printed and bound in Great Britain

Jacket front: Guildhall Square 1910
Jacket rear: Clarence Pier 1890

ACKNOWLEDGMENTS

When searching for pictures to use in a book of this nature, many come to hand for which it is impossible to credit ownership. I have, however, acknowledged every picture of which I am sure, and offer my apologies for any others not credited.

I would like to thank Geoff Salter, Miss Alison Marshall, Mr John Offord, Mr Ron Brown, Mr D.G. Dine, and the B.B.C. Hulton Picture Library for their help in supplying photographs from their collections. I am also grateful for the help and pictures given by Miss Sarah Peacock and the staff of the Portsmouth City Records Office.

Thanks must go also to Mr Nicholas Pine of Milestone Publications for giving me the opportunity of undertaking this labour of love, and to my wife Sue who has given generously of her help and encouragement.

2

INTRODUCTION

"There is no town in England which has undergone greater changes than Portsmouth during the last 60 years."

So wrote William G Gates in the foreword to his "Portsmouth in the Past", published in 1926.

Almost another 60 years have passed since those words were written, but Gates's sentiments are still true. However, since then, a second great war and modern development have again altered the shapes of roads and streets, and buildings which were once landmarks now have disappeared.

The aim of this book is to bring together a selection of scenes from Portsmouth's past, and match them with modern photographs taken from the same viewpoints.

This juxtaposition of views will give a swift and interesting comparison, showing how the streets of Portsmouth have changed.

Portsmouth has a long history, dating back to the 12th Century. There is no mention before then, although the Domesday Survey records small settlements at Buckland, Copnor, and Froddington (Fratton).

The nucleus of the town started in the area now known as Old Portsmouth, and was only a small settlement. However, in 1194 the town was considered important enough for Richard I to grant it a charter, allowing a weekly market and an annual fair.

Fortification of the town began in 1418 with the construction of the Round Tower at the entrance to the harbour. The tower is now the oldest surviving part of the fortifications.

Gradually, over the years, the fortifications were extended with the building of the Square Tower, the Great Platform, and the Long Curtain Battery. The town also boasted three gates – the Landport Gate, Quay Gate, and King James II Gate.

It was, however, with the building of the Dockyard, and its subsequent development that Portsmouth began its long spread over Portsea Island.

Although ships had been built there in an earlier period, the history of the Dockyard really dates from the reign of Henry VII, who, in 1495, ordered a dock to be built about half a mile from Portsmouth.

The yard was subsequently enlarged by Henry VIII, who has since become known as the father of the British Navy.

Portsea was virtually born in 1703, when Queen Anne granted permission to the Dockyard shipwrights to build houses on the land just outside the walls of the yard. The area was then known as Portsmouth Common. The military governor of Portsmouth, Governor Gibson, had threatened to turn his cannon on to the common if "one brick was laid on another", because he felt that any buildings would be in his line of fire should he be forced to defend the town.

The shipwrights eventually appealed to the Queen by way of her husband, Prince George, and permission was given. Queen Street and Prince George Street remain to commemorate the event.

Gradually the child outgrew the mother, and eventual development made the new Portsmouth far greater than the original town.

Portsmouth entered the canal age in 1822, with the construction of the ill-fated Portsmouth to Arundel Canal. It was drained and closed in 1827, following complaints that it was polluting the town's water supply.

The basin was situated near the present-day Commercial Road, and Arundel Street was named with the canal's eventual destination in mind. Other street names trace the waterway's path – Canal Walk, Locksway Road, and Ironbridge Lane – and, of course, the ruins of Milton Locks still can be seen.

The first railway link from Brighton to Portsmouth opened in 1847, and terminated at Portsmouth and Southsea station. The line was eventually extended to Portsmouth Harbour after the London route was completed. In 1885 a line was opened to East Southsea, but had a life of only 29 years. The line branched off from Fratton Station, and ran to East Southsea by way of two halts – Jessie Road Bridge and Highland Road Bridge. Nothing is left to record the line's passing, except for the remains of the East Southsea station concourse, which still stands in the grounds of a garage in Granada Road.

The tramway began in 1865, and the service linked Portsmouth and Southsea station with Clarence Pier, to serve the Isle of Wight ferry service. Electricity came to the city in 1894, and by 1903 the first electric trams replaced the horse-drawn ones. The last tram ran in 1936, when the trolley-bus service came into operation.

Portsmouth was still growing, and by 1904 the whole of Portsea Island was included in the borough, and the area to the east of Old Portsmouth, which had been popular as a residential area for Army and Navy officers, began to develop into the holiday resort of today.

After the first world war other changes were made. Cosham was incorporated into the borough in 1920, and by 1926 the town was raised to the dignity of a city. The parish church of St. Thomas's at Old Portsmouth became the new cathedral.

Between the years 1927 and 1930 a massive slum clearance operation was carried out at Portsea. Many of the wretched little streets, including the notorious White's Row and Blossom Alley, were demolished, and new council homes were built.

Until the war years the only road connecting the island to the mainland was the one over Portsbridge. The present bridge replaced the old iron swing bridge in 1927, when much of the old fortifications, known as the Hilsea Lines, were demolished. In 1941 a second link was made when the Eastern Road was completed.

In 1929 Fratton Road was widened at a cost of £89,000. Elm Grove was widened in 1930, in 1932 Northern Parade was opened, and in the same year the city's airport started operations.

After the blitz of the second world war, the face of the city changed yet again, leading to the modern Portsmouth of today, with its wide roads and pedestrian precincts.

The old pictures in this book are divided roughly by date into two periods. Half were taken at the turn of the century, while the remaining date from the thirties, which, after all, is half a century ago.

Perhaps in 50 years time some future compiler of a similar book will use my modern photographs as his "past". It would be interesting to know how the face of Portsmouth will look then.

Anthony Triggs,

4

CONTENTS

SOUTH PARADE PIER – 1900 *The original pier was opened in 1879, with the aim of attracting Isle of Wight ferry custom. Because of the shelving beach, the pier was a long one — 400 yards. It was supposed to be fire-proof, but nevertheless was destroyed in a blaze in 1904.*

SOUTH PARADE PIER – 1984 *The new pier was completed in 1908, and included a theatre in the main building. Eight hundred men were hired for a day to jump about on the planking to test its stability. The superstructure was altered yet again when a serious fire, during the filming of "Tommy" in 1974, almost caused history to repeat itself.*

HANDLEYS' CORNER – 1935 *Handleys was opened in 1867, and eventually became the most fashionable store in Southsea. The shop is pictured decorated to celebrate the Silver Jubilee of King George V and Queen Mary.*

HANDLEYS' CORNER – 1984   *Handleys is now part of a national chain. The store is decorated once more, this time for the fortieth anniversary of D-Day. The shop now stands on the corner of Palmerston Road and Osborne Road, not Portland Road, which was realigned after the blitz.*

OSBORNE ROAD – 1933   *The camera is looking down Osborne Road, and the road entering the picture on the right is Portland Road, before realignment. It is interesting to note the sign above the shop on the left — Bright's Corner — perhaps the owners were in competition with the store in the previous pair of pictures.*

OSBORNE ROAD – 1984 *Portland Road now joins Osborne Road higher up on the right. Bright's shop was destroyed in the war, and the corner is now occupied by a bank.*

11

GROVE ROAD SOUTH – 1907   *This view of Grove Road South exactly depicts the slow pace of early Edwardian times. An early guide book described it as "perhaps the most shady and rural" in Southsea.*

GROVE ROAD SOUTH – 1984 *Today Grove Road South is a busy thoroughfare. The buildings on the right are now the St. John's College complex, although the stone gatepost still remains.*

ELM GROVE – 1880 *Elm Grove was aptly named in those days. However, the rural solitude was not to last long, and against a barrage of complaints from residents, many of the villas were demolished to make way for shops.*

ELM GROVE – 1984 *Elm Grove is now almost entirely made up of shops, and the villas and trees of the previous picture are now things of the past.*

ELM GROVE – 1929 *Elm Grove was a popular shopping area by this time, but some of the residential properties can be seen on the right of the picture.*

ELM GROVE – 1984   *The change is not a dramatic one, although the trees have unfortunately disappeared. The residential properties eventually became offices for members of the legal professions.*

KINGS ROAD – 1900   *The Bush Hotel stood on the corner of Kings Road and Elm Grove. Sherlock Holmes was created in No 1 Bush Villas, which is the building sandwiched between the hotel and the church. It was here that Doctor Conan Doyle practised, from 1882 to 1890.*

KINGS ROAD – 1984 *Almost the entire Kings Road shopping centre was destroyed in the war. The block of flats on the right is named Bush House, and recently the Sherlock Holmes Society of London paid for a plaque, in memory of the "great detective", to be placed on the outside wall.*

CLARENCE ESPLANADE – 1900   *Clarence Esplanade, named after the then Lieutenant-Governor of Portsmouth, Lord Frederick Fitzclarence, was commenced in 1848, and soon became popular among holidaymakers.*

20

CLARENCE ESPLANADE – 1984 *The hovercraft terminal now is the main attraction for visitors. The hovercraft itself offers a far speedier crossing to the Isle of Wight, than did the boats of 80 years ago.*

21

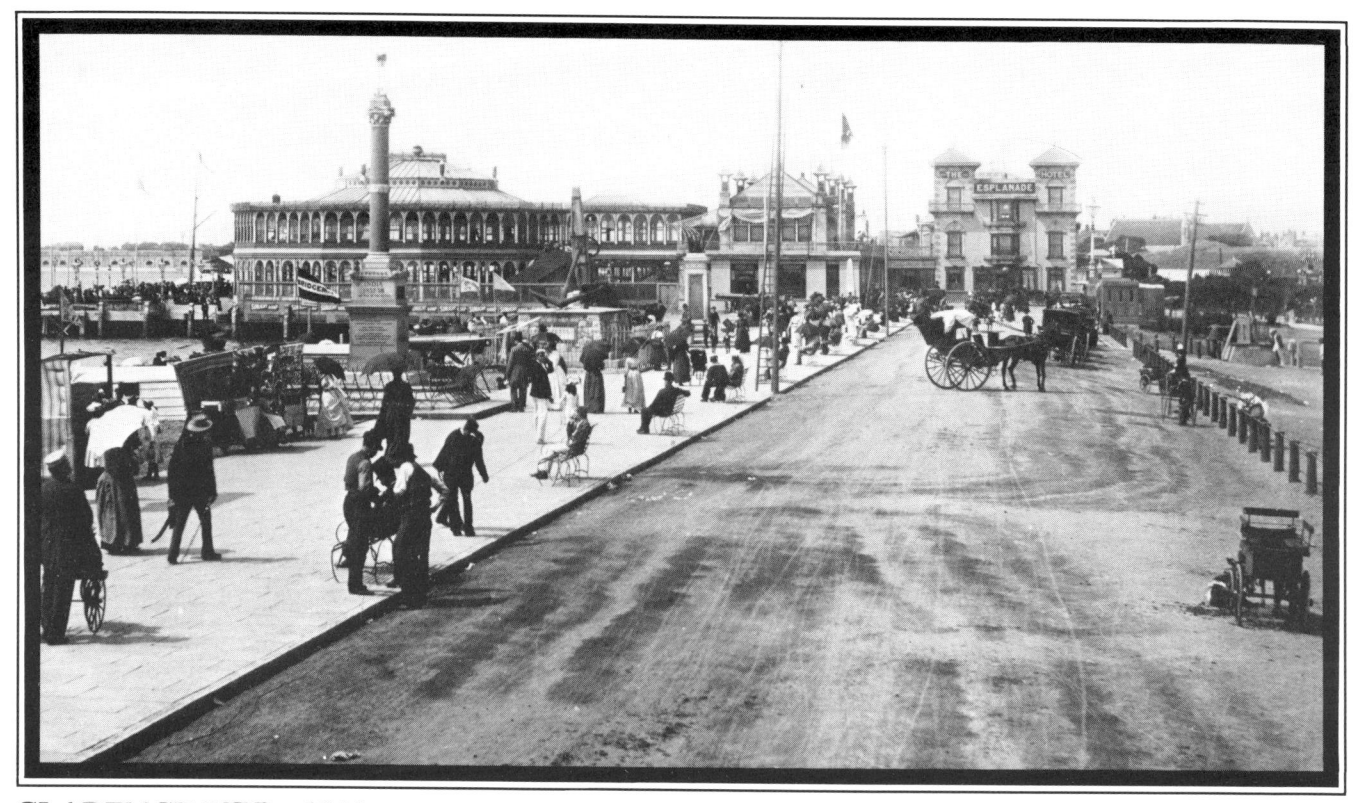

CLARENCE PIER – 1900   *Clarence Pier was opened in 1861, and provided band shows and concerts. It became more popular in 1886, when the tramway link to the Town station was opened.*

CLARENCE PIER – 1984 *The pier suffered much damage during the war, but was reopened in 1961, after extensive rebuilding. A few boat trips are still available from the pier, although the hovercraft, just next door, has probably killed much of that trade.*

ESPLANADE HOTEL – 1933 *The Esplanade Hotel was converted in 1877 from the former King's Rooms, originally built in 1816 as assembly rooms and baths. The last duel fought by Englishmen on their native soil arose from a quarrel between two officers at a ball at the King's Rooms.*

SITE OF ESPLANADE HOTEL – 1984   *The hotel and pier entrance were destroyed in the war, and the resultant buildings are of the typical seaside variety — bars, seafood stalls, and gift shops — with the pleasure of the funfair just behind them.*

PIER ROAD – 1910   *Pier Road was a tram turning point, and a popular place, especially so when the circus was in town. The Victoria Barracks dominate the skyline.* (Portsmouth City Records Office)

PIER ROAD – 1984 *The road has now lost some open space, and has gained some trees, but it is still a popular route from the city to Clarence Pier.*

KING WILLIAM GATE – 1850   *This was the last, and the least ornate, of the gates of Old Portsmouth. It was built in 1834 to give access to the Southsea area. The pathway for pedestrians was so tortuous that it became known as the "Crooked Arch".* (BBC Hulton Picture Library)

SITE OF KING WILLIAM GATE – 1984   *The gate was demolished in 1876. The guardhouse of the gate still stands in Pembroke Road, and can be seen on the left of the picture. The ornate frontage of the Royal Naval Club, with its tower, still adds an item of historic splendour to the road.*

VICTORIA AVENUE – 1900   *This commercial postcard view shows the officers' quarters of the Victoria Barracks, which were built in 1880. The construction work was done by convicts, and there is a story which tells of the man who did the carvings on the apex at each end of the building, asked to be kept in prison after his sentence so that he could complete the work.*

30

VICTORIA AVENUE – 1984   *The barracks were last used as a Naval training establishment, and were eventually demolished in the sixties. A housing development called Pembroke Park, and the Crest Hotel, formerly the Centre Hotel, were built on the site.*

SOUTHSEA TERRACE – 1890   *The Pier Hotel stands proud and new in Southsea Terrace, when that part of Portsmouth was in its hey-day as a high class residential area.*

SOUTHSEA TERRACE – 1984 *The hotel still stands, although it has had various lives since the previous picture was taken. It is now used as students' accommodation.*

BROAD STREET – 1930   *The public house on the right, The Old Blue Posts, replaced a previous one of the same name, which was destroyed in 1870. The original inn was made famous by Marryatt, for it was here that midshipmen would "leave their chestesses", and would forget "to pay for their breakfastesses"*

BROAD STREET – 1984   *The quaint houses still stand on the west side, and the docks and their associated industries seem to have taken over the east. This was also the approximate site of the Old King James's Gate, one of the original entrances to Portsmouth.*

HIGH STREET – 1875   *High Street in its dignified days, with the George Hotel in the centre of the view. The hotel was famous as the last place on British soil that Nelson stayed, before leaving for Trafalgar.* (BBC Hulton Picture Library)

HIGH STREET – 1984   *High Street is now largely residential. The George Hotel is now only remembered by George Court, a block of flats standing on the site, although the two lamp-posts on the pavement remain.*

HIGH STREET – 1933   *This was the view, looking across to the entrance to Portsmouth Cathedral. The shops were soon to disappear with the extension of the Cathedral green.*

HIGH STREET – 1984   *The open aspect of the green of today gives the Cathedral space to show itself off to best advantage.*

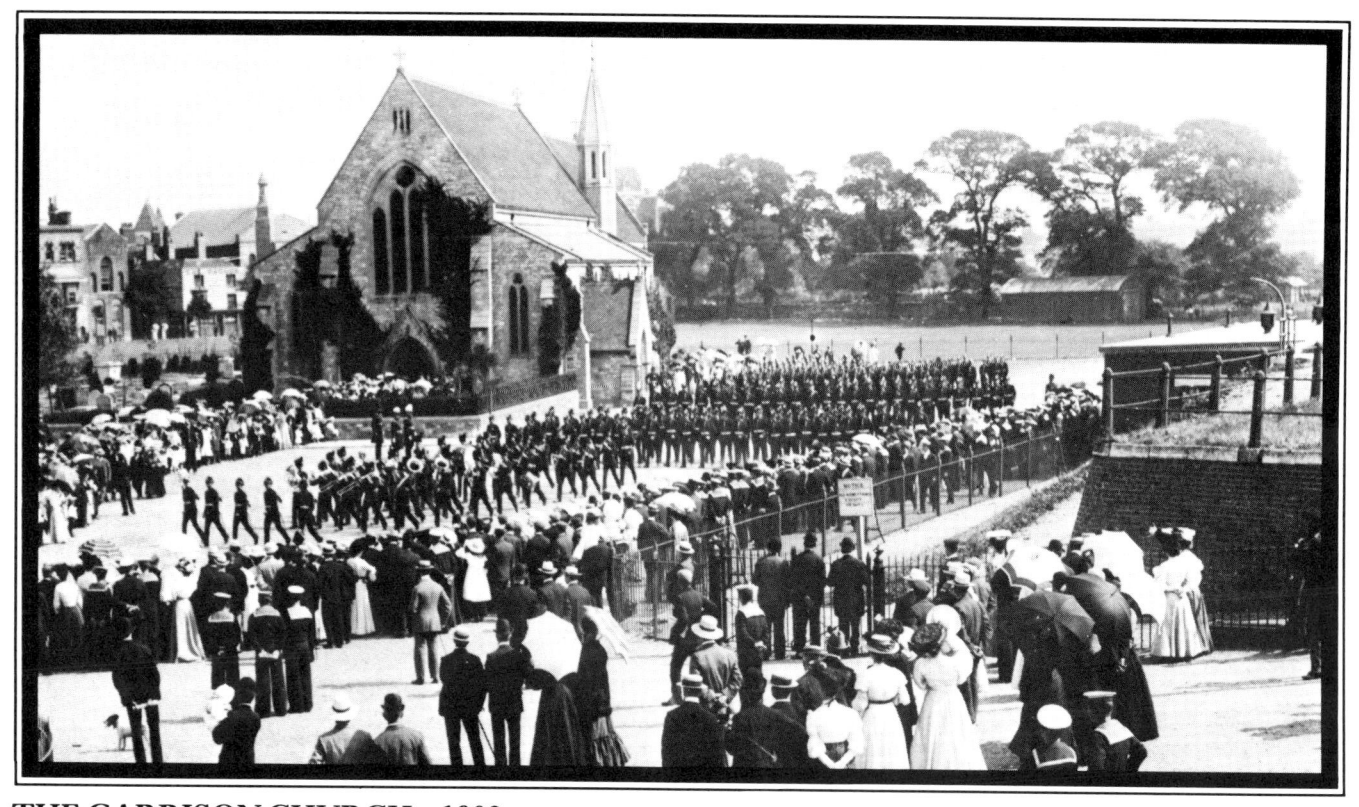

THE GARRISON CHURCH – 1902   *Easter Sunday church parade in 1902. The Garrison Church is the last remains of the Domus Dei, or God's House, founded in 1212 as a hospital.*

THE GARRISON CHURCH – 1984   *The church was hit by a bomb in 1941, which destroyed the nave. Now the building is an ancient monument.*

CAMBRIDGE ROAD – 1900 *A horse tram is seen negotiating the junction of Cambridge Road and High Street. The Grammar School building in the background was opened in 1879.* (BBC Hulton Picture Library)

42

CAMBRIDGE ROAD – 1984   *The junction has developed more trees since the previous picture. The road to the left is now named Museum Road.*

THE HARD – 1900   *This area of Portsmouth was once known as the "Devil's Acre", because of the large number of beer houses and inns. In later years the Hard was home for the mudlarks — youngsters who would dive into the black mud for coppers thrown by passers-by.*

THE HARD – 1984   *Many of the buildings remain, although the ferry terminus dominates the area. This picture was taken through a window of the covered walkway linking the Harbour station with the Hard.*

45

PORTSMOUTH HARBOUR – 1915   *This commercial postcard view, taken from the ferry pontoon, shows the South Railway Jetty, where the battleship is moored, and the viaduct linking it with Portsmouth Harbour Station. (Ron Brown)*

PORTSMOUTH HARBOUR – 1984   *The viaduct was demolished in 1960. The new ferry boats came into service in 1966, and gave passengers a more comfortable and sheltered journey to and from Gosport.*

QUEEN STREET – 1900   *This photograph, by F J Mortimer, was taken in April, 1900, and captures the scene as Queen Street prepared to welcome H.M.S. Powerful on her return from the Boer War. The ladder, in the centre of the picture, is resting against the Royal Sailors' Home Club, which was opened in 1851.* (BBC Hulton Picture Library)

QUEEN STREET – 1984   *Queen Street today presents a different picture. The modern wide road bears no resemblance to the narrow thoroughfare of the previous view, although the Royal Sailors' Home Club is still there, but in a modern building.*

COMMERCIAL ROAD – 1912   *This view, with the Theatre Royal on the left, looks down towards the Guildhall Square, where can be seen the railway bridge and the Portsmouth and Southsea station.* (Portsmouth City Records Office)

COMMERCIAL ROAD – 1984   *This title is not now strictly true, as the road has been renamed Guildhall Walk. However, the Theatre Royal is still standing, but the station is now hidden behind the glass and steel of the Civic Offices.*

COMMERCIAL ROAD – 1930 *This view, looking towards the Guildhall, shows Edinburgh Road to the right, and Arundel Street running out to the left by the Landport Drapery Bazaar.*

COMMERCIAL ROAD – 1984 *The Commercial Road shopping centre is now a pedestrian precinct, and part of Arundel Street has been realigned. The fountain, decorated with the Queen's Beasts, was completed in 1977, and is now a popular place in hot weather.*

COMMERCIAL ROAD – 1905 *This picture captures exactly the slow pace of the early part of the century. Charlotte Street turns off to the right of the picture, and it is interesting to note that the jewellery firm of H Samuel has premises where they still stand today.* (Portsmouth City Records Office)

COMMERCIAL ROAD – 1984 *The familiar view of today's Commercial Road is a contrast to the earlier picture, although the line of the buildings on the left are still as they were nearly 100 years ago.*

GUILDHALL SQUARE – 1933   *This view, taken from the steps of the Guildhall, shows the Portsmouth and Southsea station goods depot, with the trams and trolleys in Greetham Street, to the right.*

GUILDHALL SQUARE – 1984   *Taken from approximately the same position, this picture shows a completely contrasting view. The tinted glass of the Civic Offices, which were opened in 1976, dominates the scene, reflecting the majesty of the Guildhall.*

THE GUILDHALL – 1930   *The Guildhall was opened in 1890 by the Prince of Wales, later Edward VII, and was built to the design of Bolton Town Hall. Queen Victoria stands among the trees, and between her and the Guildhall is the tram shelter.*

THE GUILDHALL – 1984   *After suffering damage during the war, the Guildhall was reopened by the Queen in 1959. Modern development makes an identical view impossible, but in the square the tram shelter has gone, as have the trees and the Guildhall minarets.*

LAKE ROAD – 1900   *Lake Road was once known as Lake Lane, and was so named because an arm of the sea ran thus far until the 15th Century. The building behind the tram is the famous Princes Theatre.* (John Offord)

60

LAKE ROAD – 1984   *The Princes Theatre eventually became a cinema, and was destroyed in August 1940. The tiny shops of later years have all been replaced by modern council flats.*

GOLDSMITH AVENUE – 1909 *This view, taken from the window of the Talbot Hotel, shows tram lines being laid. Part of the road ran along the bed of the Portsmouth to Arundel Canal, as did some of the railway. The line to East Southsea can be seen running beneath the bridge.* (Portsmouth City Records Office)

GOLDSMITH AVENUE – 1984   *The railway to East Southsea closed in 1914, and the Goldsmith Avenue Bridge, along with the Jessie Road Bridge and Highland Road Bridge, was demolished in 1926, when the road was straightened. After the trams stopped in 1936, the lines were taken up.*

FRATTON ROAD – 1929 *The newly-widened Fratton Road was officially opened on July 22, 1929, and this picture shows the Mayoral procession going towards Fratton Bridge.*

FRATTON ROAD – 1984   *The view has not changed a great deal, although Co-operative House, on the left, has been burned down and rebuilt since the previous picture was taken. The date 1928, the year before the opening, can be seen above the shop on the right.*

FRATTON ROAD – 1900   *This view shows a horse-tram passing St. Mary's Church, in a far slower and more peaceful age. Another picture which demonstrates the skill of the Victorian photographer.* (BBC Hulton Picture Library)

FRATTON ROAD – 1984 *St. Mary's Church, of course, still stands, but the tombs and tramlines have disappeared with the years.*

FRATTON POLICE STATION – 1926   *This imposing police and fire station was closed and demolished when the new Kingston Crescent police headquarters were opened in 1965.*

SITE OF FRATTON POLICE STATION – 1984   *The station now has been replaced with a modern health centre to serve the growing community in the area. The Museum Gardens public house is still standing.*

SOMERS ROAD – 1932   *A wet day in Somers Road. Not an inspiring view, but typical of many streets in that part of the city.*

SOMERS ROAD – 1984 *Some of the old shops still remain, but the area covered by this view shows a marked difference to that of the previous picture.*

GAMBLE ROAD – 1929 *This picture presents a more depressing view of the late twenties, although the entire area was soon to change in a comprehensive road-widening scheme.*

GAMBLE ROAD – 1984 *The Gamble Road of today has completely changed, and Bedford Street has disappeared.*

FRATTON ROAD – 1929 *This view looks northwards to Kingston Cross. The Tramway Arms public house marked the junction of Lake Road with Fratton Road.*

74

FRATTON ROAD – 1984 *Development has changed this view. Lake Road has been realigned, and now joins Fratton Road to the immediate left of the picture.*

KINGSTON CRESCENT – 1935   *This view shows Kingston Crescent from Commercial Road, looking towards North End and Kingston Road. Chapman's Laundry can be seen, hidden behind the houses in the middle of the picture.*

KINGSTON CRESCENT – 1984   *Development has dramatically changed this part of Portsmouth, although the laundry premises are still on the same site, and many of the houses past the laundry are still standing.*

LONDON ROAD, NORTH END – 1929 *This is North End when it was a prosperous shopping centre. The photograph was taken in June, which was obviously warm, judging from the number of shop awnings on show.*

LONDON ROAD, NORTH END – 1984 *Surprisingly little has changed from the previous view. The tobacconists' and* Boots the Chemist still have premises in the same positions

NORTH END JUNCTION – 1900 *This contemporary postcard shows the junction with London Road and Gladys Avenue. The large house was known as "The Poplars".* (D.G. Dine)

NORTH END JUNCTION – 1984   *The junction today shows a different view, with the National bus company's office replacing the house. The Gladys Avenue bus depot was demolished only a short while before this picture was taken.*

TWYFORD AVENUE – 1930   *This picture show the junction of Twyford Avenue and Kingston Crescent, which leads out to the right. The Methodist church on the left was so badly damaged by fire in 1971, that it had to be demolished.*

TWYFORD AVENUE – 1984 *The new multi-lane highway has completely obliterated this end of Twyford Avenue. The public house on the right originally stood in the line of buildings past the horse and cart in the previous picture. Now it stands alone.*

HIGH STREET, COSHAM – 1904   *This attractive view by Waterlooville photographer C.H.T. Marshall, shows the High Street in those slower days, when the sight of a camera aroused a deal of interest.* (Miss A Marshall)

84

HIGH STREET, COSHAM – 1984 *The shop in the centre stands now on the corner of High Street and Wayte Street. In the previous picture it stood on the corner of Southampton Road, which has now been realigned.*

LONDON ROAD, HILSEA – 1910 *The tram lines, with their electric power lines above, are seen running to the only exit from Portsea Island, through the fortifications known as the Hilsea Lines. It is interesting to note the royal cypher above the arches.* (Portsmouth City Records Office)

LONDON ROAD, HILSEA – 1984 *How different is the view of today. The multi-lane highway now brings in traffic on a scale undreamed of in 1910, and the motorway in the background could never have been imagined.*

LONDON ROAD, HILSEA – 1923   *This picture faces south along London Road, and shows the Hilsea Lines being demolished, prior to the building of the road on the new Portsbridge, in 1927.*

LONDON ROAD, HILSEA – 1984 *The same view presents a marked difference, although the site of the filling station was occupied in the earlier picture. The entrance arch to the Portsmouth Grammar School playing fields, seen clearly in 1923, is still standing, but has been repositioned away from the road.*

NORTHERN ROAD, COSHAM – 1934 *This picture really portrays the wide open spaces of the thirties. The large building with the arched windows, just to the left of the road is the old Cosham post office.*

NORTHERN ROAD COSHAM – 1984 *Viewed from the telephone exchange, the scene is rather different. The new post office replaced the old one in 1958.*

PORTSDOWN HILL – 1930   *This picture was taken at Easter of that year, and shows the popular fair on the hill slopes.*

PORTSDOWN HILL – 1984 *In later years the fair moved to a higher position on the hill, and houses began to encroach upon the lower slopes.*

PORTSDOWN HILL – 1905 *This picture, another by C.H.T. Marshall, shows a tram of the Portsdown and Horndean Light Railway negotiating the gradient at the George Inn. The tea rooms on the left were demolished in 1957. (Miss A Marshall)*

PORTSDOWN HILL – 1984   *The George still stands amidst the modern road junctions and fly-overs. The houses behind the inn have since disappeared, but more trees have appeared.*

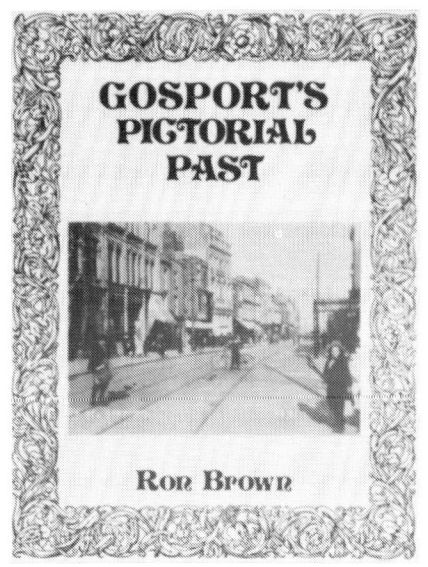

Gosport's Pictorial Past

Ron Brown

A nostalgic reminder of Gosport, Alverstoke and Lee-on-the-Solent during the past 100 years. The book provides an attractive pictorial record illustrating the people, the businesses, the buildings, the military and the day to day life in the Gosport of yesteryear.

253mm × 195mm, 96 pages, 168 b/w photographs.

Hardback   £6.95

Portsmouth's Pictorial Past

Ron Brown

A fascinating pictorial record of life in Portsmouth between 1875 and 1941. Places, faces, events, street scenes, modes of transport, businesses and the Royal Navy are featured in the 170 photographs which are all accompanied by descriptive text.

253mm × 195mm, 96 pages, 170 b/w photographs.

Hardback   £6.95

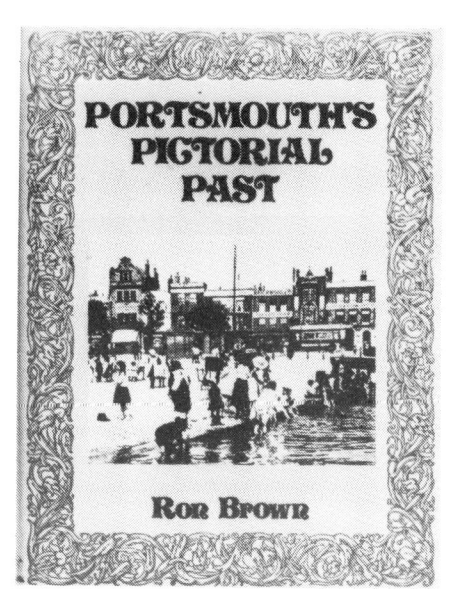